I. INTRODUCTION

The Federal Trade Commission (FTC) is an administrative agency charged, along with the Department of Justice (DOJ), with enforcing the antitrust laws. However, unlike the DOJ, the FTC litigates the antitrust cases it chooses to prosecute, known as "administrative complaints", in front of its own administrative law judges (ALJs), and then hears the appeal itself. While this process has raised concerns in the past (Posner (1969), ABA (1989)), it has been subject to little empirical investigation.

This study focuses on the formal decisions made by the FTC after an ALJ has conducted a full trial on the merits for a particular case. The analysis explores a number of issues with a data set generated by surveying all of the FTC's merger decisions from the 1950 reform of the Clayton Act to 1992. In particular, the structure of the FTC raises a number of interesting questions concerning how the institution actually responds to various internal and external pressures.

Our study finds that while the merits of a particular matter affect the commission's decision, internal political factors also matter. In particular, the number of commissioners who both vote to prosecute and then vote as a judge in a case impacts on the FTC's decision, as well as the political affiliation of the commissioners. Contrary to previous studies, however, we find little evidence of an external political effect on FTC judicial decisions.

II. THE FTC'S ADMINISTRATIVE PROCESS

The FTC enforces the antitrust laws in partnership with the DOJ. Much of the antitrust casework involves the evaluation of the competitive effects of proposed and consummated mergers. Decisions are made by a majority vote of the five Commissioners, in response to staff recommendations on particular cases. Commissioners are appointed by the President and confirmed by the Senate for terms of up to seven years.

If the merging firms choose to oppose an FTC enforcement action, the agency initiates a lengthy court process to attempt to obtain a permanent injunction against the merger.[1] After presiding at a trial on the merits, the ALJ issues an initial decision and an order to remedy any identified problems. This decision and any ensuing order may be appealed to the Commission by either the respondents or the FTC staff. The Commission then issues a "formal" decision on the merits, along with an order to resolve the competitive concern. The FTC decision can incorporate a complete review of the trial record, and is not constrained in any way by the findings of the ALJ.[2] If the Commission finds a violation, the respondents may appeal to a federal appeals court and, ultimately to the Supreme Court before an order is actually enforced.[3]

In effect, the administrative FTC is transformed into a federal court for the purpose of ruling on a merger. Along the lines of Cohen (1991), we expect that, in making these decisions, FTC commissioners can be modeled as utility-maximizers. We hypothesize that FTC administrative decision making on mergers is driven by three different types of factors. The first set of factors is the actual merits of a particular matter. Given the possibility of appeal, and that a reversal on appeal would diminish the reputation of commissioners, the stronger the merits of a case, the more likely the FTC is to

---

[1] Under the 1976 Hart-Scott-Rodino (HSR) Act, the FTC can also interdict a proposed merger by obtaining a preliminary injunction from a federal district court, with possible review from the relevant court of appeals. If the court declines to issue the injunction, the firms are free to merge, subject to the administrative process described here. Between October 1983 and September 1992, the FTC voted to challenge 75 horizontal mergers filed under Hart-Scott-Rodino. The Commission litigated 13 of these cases in federal court, winning ten injunctions. Administrative complaints coincided with the injunctions, although most of the defendants settled and abandoned their transactions. In the five cases that went to trial, the Commission dismissed one, ordered a divestiture in another and settled a third after a Commission decision on the merits. One is currently on appeal although the acquisition collapsed years ago and the last is at the Commission for a decision. Thus, only one or at most two of the 75 transactions will have survived the FTC process under the HSR Act.

[2] The DOJ uses the federal court system for merger law enforcement. While a preliminary injunction trial would be similar to one litigated by the FTC, the DOJ also can litigate cases against consummated mergers in a full trial on the merits. In recent years, however, the DOJ has started litigating combined preliminary injunction/full trials on the merits. This approach allows the court system to rule on the legality of a merger in a one step process.

[3] We note that it has now been over twenty years since the Supreme Court decided a merger case on the merits, *U.S. vs. General Dynamics* 415 U.S. 486 (1974).

rule favorably for itself and against the relevant firms in a particular matter. We expect horizontal merger cases to be stronger than vertical or potential competition cases, holding other structural factors constant. It is also possible that the FTC's merger enforcement standards have changed over time, with more recent cases less likely to lead to merger orders, again holding other considerations constant. In particular, the Supreme Court's 1974 *General Dynamics* decision may have had an effect on the process, because the court ruled that merger decisions must look beyond market concentration and into other competitive aspects of a merger case.

The second factor is how a case fits into the internal political structure at the FTC. This could be especially important given the process by which FTC complaints are decided. Complaints are first voted out by FTC commissioners and are then sent for trial before an ALJ, who is also an FTC employee. Once the ALJ makes his decision, the case is appealed back to the Commission, a commission often consisting of some of the same people who issued the complaint in the first place. Thus, unlike most of the American legal system, an FTC commissioner can be both the prosecutor and the judge on a particular case.[4] Utility-maximizing commissioners may well be reluctant to publicly admit they were mistaken in prosecuting a particular matter. We hypothesize that the more commissioners voting on a formal decision who were also part of the decision to prosecute that matter, the more likely it is that the FTC will find in favor of its own case.

The Commissioners' political affiliations may also influence their decisions, with Republican commissioners hypothesized to be less likely to support cases than Democratic commissioners, all else equal. This hypothesis questions the "public interest" model of antitrust, because it claims politics affects antitrust decisions. However, if one admits to different interpretations of the "public interest", one can argue that Democratic and Republican commissioners are simply voting ideologically different

---

[4] The 1989 American Bar Association (ABA) committee report on the Federal Trade Commission noted "no thoughtful observer is entirely comfortable with the FTC's (or other agencies') combining the prosecutory and adjudicatory functions. Whenever the same people who issued a complaint later decide whether it should be dismissed, concern about at least the appearance of fairness is inevitable (ABA 1989 at 35)". However, only a minority of the ABA committee recommended reform to separate the functions.

interpretations of the public interest.[5] For example, a disagreement over the goals of antitrust would generate different voting patterns. Republicans could support an economic efficiency standard which would allow for limited enforcement, while Democrats could support a consumers' surplus standard which would lead to more aggressive enforcement.[6] The political variable could be driven either by the nominal party affiliation of the Commissioner or the party of the President making the appointment. It may be possible to determine if the FTC Act has been successful in achieving a "balanced" commission with Republican Presidents actually appointing "true" Democrats and Democratic Presidents appointing "true" Republicans.

The third factor that could affect FTC decisions is outside political influence. The FTC is an administrative agency funded by Congress, and thus may be affected by the make-up of its oversight bodies. Standard public choice theory, along the lines of Weingast and Moran (1983), indicates that the Commission will be reluctant to offend Congress because doing so could reduce the FTC's funding. We expect that the more "liberal" the various Congressional bodies are, the more likely the commission will be to find an antitrust violation in order to protect commission financing. Also, it may be that if larger firms have political influence, the FTC could be less likely to rule against such firms.

Politics could also enter the analysis more directly. The FTC could be less likely to find against firms if such firms are located in the district of a Congressman or Senator serving on an FTC oversight committee or subcommittee. Previously, Faith, Leavens, and Tollison (1982) found support for a "pork barrel" hypothesis through analyzing the correlation between FTC decisions and membership on FTC oversight committees. This paper will test the "pork barrel" hypothesis by looking for a relationship between the identity of the members on the various oversight committees and the outcome of the case.

---

[5] Contrast this observation with the work linking enforcement decisions to politics during the Reagan/Bush commission (see Coate, Higgins and McChesney, 1990). While the political composition of the Commission varied significantly from 1956 to 1988, the political composition of the Reagan/Bush commission changed little. Thus, changes in enforcement intensity linked to exogenous political variables is more difficult to explain away as a difference of opinion.

[6] These examples are for illustrative purposes; any difference in interpretation of the goals of antitrust would generate hypothesized results.

III. OVERVIEW OF THE DATA

A. Relevant Variables

The data set was constructed by reviewing all mergers challenged by the FTC from 1950 to 1988 and decided between 1956 and 1992. After excluding three mergers because the relevant acquisition was a small part of a broad antitrust case, four mergers because the challenged transactions were designed to restructure an industry, three mergers because the staff withdrew their challenge during the litigation and one merger case because it was closed on non-economic grounds, we were left with a sample of 70 mergers. Of the 70 cases, 44 were horizontal, 12 were vertical and 14 dealt with potential competition theories.[7]

All of these transactions went through the same basic process. The Commission initiated action challenging the various transactions by issuing a formal complaint, a trial was held and an ALJ decision issued, usually a couple of years after the formal complaint. Then the case was argued before the Commission and an official decision was issued.

With respect to the economic merits of a particular matter, the FTC decisions contained information on the key economic issues of concentration and entry barriers. We used the Herfindahl index (Herfindahl) as the relevant measure of concentration. This figure was taken directly from the recent decisions and calculated from market share information for old decisions.[8] The decisions also

_____

[7] Of the seven excluded merger cases, five were horizontal mergers, one was a vertical transaction and one was a potential competition matter. The four industry cases involved both horizontal and potential competition issues. Complaints issued after 1988 are generally still working their way through the legal system.

[8] In most cases, either the shares of the top 8 firms were recorded or four and eight firm concentration ratios were given along with a few actual share figures. In this case, the missing share figures would be estimated from the concentration data. While complete universe of data was not available, fringe shares were estimated from the residual. Given the Herfindahl is driven by the large share firms, only minimal error should be introduced. For nine cases, the Herfindahl was estimated from the four-firm concentration ratio using a mapping defined by the Coate, Higgins and McChesney (1990) data set. Finally, in four industries, the decisions noted the government failed to prove a market and no Herfindahl finding was made. These missing values were assigned the value 1000 (along the lines of the DOJ 1992 (and 1982) Guidelines' "unconcentrated" threshold) to indicate an unconcentrated market.

included barrier-to-entry findings (Barriers) usually in the FTC decision, though a few cases contained only barrier information in the ALJ decision. In recent cases, the finding was highlighted as an explicit part of the analysis, while in older cases, the information tended to be mentioned as an aside. As a check on this variable, the authors reviewed the specific industries involved in the transactions. While a few of the barrier determinations appeared incorrect (i.e. most observers would likely considered entry easy into the florist foil market in the 1990's), the great majority of the determinations appeared valid under Merger Guideline principles elucidated during the 1980's.) Of course, disputes would remain, with some believing entry to be easy in retailing, various brand name consumer products and distribution, while others would offer more sophisticated explanations for why entry would be deterred. Although the historical decisions tend to resolve disputes with a finding of entry barriers, no clear shift in policy was identified.[9] In our model, the merits of a merger case depend on both the level of the Herfindahl and the presence of barriers to entry. As the Herfindahl increases, we expect the Commission to be more likely to find a violation. Likewise, the Commission would be more likely to enjoin a transaction if barriers to entry existed.

We also computed a time trend variable, defined in months and starting from January 1956, the year of the first FTC decision in our data series. The April 1974 date of the *General Dynamics* decision is of particular interest, because this Supreme Court decision increased the burden on the government in merger cases. An interaction of the time trend with a dummy variable associated with the date of the *General Dynamics* decision would take on a negative sign if merger standards tended to be gradually relaxed following the Supreme Court's decision.

Throughout the period in question, not only did the Commission deal with pure horizontal mergers, but it also dealt with vertical mergers and mergers dealing with issues of potential competition. To account for these different types of cases, we defined a variable equal to 1 if the matter involves a vertical acquisition, and zero otherwise, and a variable equal to 1 if the matter deals with potential

---

[9] Evidence on competitive conditions and efficiencies were noted in recent cases, but were often omitted entirely in the older cases. Thus, no attempt was made to collect this data.

competition, and zero otherwise. Given these cases are generally considered less threatening to competition than horizontal mergers (holding the structure variable constant), we expect a negative sign for both variables.

For internal political factors, background information on the FTC was also collected. First, the initial complaint and the final decision, are linked with an index OLD for the number of Commissioners that both served on the Commission when the complaint was issued and subsequently voted on the final decision. This index ranges from 0 to 5. Consistent with Posner (1969), we expect that the number of OLD commissioners deciding a matter will have a systematic positive effect on the Commission's final decision. We expect that Commissioners who voted to prosecute a particular matter will be, on average, reluctant to admit, by finding for the parties in that matter, that the decision to prosecute could have been a mistake.[10]

To obtain some understanding of the partisan political influences inside the Commission, two political variables were computed at the time of the official decision.[11] The first variable (Republican) estimates the average political affiliation of the Commission, with the value 1 assigned to each Republican Commissioner and the value zero to each Democratic Commissioner voting in the decision.[12] Although the Commission is only allowed to have three members from a party, the fact that some Commission seats temporarily become empty and that some Commissioners do not participate in particular manners allows the index to exhibit a somewhat wider range (from 0.25 to 0.75 in the sample). A second index (President) considers a commissioner to be associated with the party of the

---

[10] Another interpretation of such a result is that both prosecutions and final orders may in part represent idiosyncrasies of particular commissioners. If this were the case, the FTC administrative process could be seen as not have the normal checks against idiosyncrasies of a standard court system.

[11] The political index for the Commissioners issuing a decision was based on the Commissioners participating in the matter.

[12] Independent Commissioners are assigned to the party with the minority at the Commission. One "independent" Commission Elizabeth Hanford is considered to have switched parties, counting initially as a Democrat (to avoid a Republican share of 80 percent) and then as a Republican (to avoid a Democratic share of 80 percent). She married Republican Senator Robert Dole while on the Commission.

President that made that Commissioner's initial appointment. We set this variable equal to the percentage of the Commission appointed by a Republican president. This variable ranges from 0 in the mid 1960's to 1 in the late 1980's. If Republican commissioners are less likely to support merger regulation, a negative sign would be observed for at least one of the variables. In theory, if the President is able to appoint individuals sympathetic to the position of his party, independent of a commissioner's formal affiliation, the variable for the party of the appointing President will be more significant, while if the appointed commissioners are more likely to represent party positions at the Commission, the official party affiliation variable will be more important.

For external political factors, consistent with much previous literature (for example, Weingast and Moran, 1983), we use the "liberal quotient", as measured by the group Americans for Democratic Action (ADA), for the FTC congressional oversight committees, subcommittees, subcommittee chairmen, as well as for Congress as a whole. We expect that the more liberal the median member of the relevant House and Senate oversight bodies are, the more likely the commission is to take an activist role and find for itself in a particular matter. However, we do not know if the influence resides at the full house level or is generated in the committee system. To test for various possibilities, we use, along the lines of Spiller and Gely (1992), ratings at four levels: subcommittee chairman, subcommittee, committee, and the full house.

We also hypothesize that the size of the respondent firms matters. It is possible that large firms may bring more political pressure to bear on the FTC to rule in their favor. Another way of interpreting such an effect, as McChesney (1991) suggests, is that decisions in favor of large firms may represent rent-extraction on the part of the FTC. On the other hand, large firms may be targets for "populist" antitrust and thus be more likely to lose. Two measures of size, the sales of the acquiring firm and the value of the transaction were considered. Most of the cases contained information on both the dollar value of the merger transaction and the sales of the acquiring firm. If the value was not reported, the Wall Street Journal index was used to search for the actual value. Likewise, if the sales of the acquiring firm were missing, various corporate indexes were consulted. The values were transformed to real prices with the GNP price deflator.[13] Logarithmic transformations were also considered to allow for a declining effect associated with increases in size.

Finally, we test to see if the pork barrel hypothesis applies to FTC decisions. We gathered data on the jurisdictions of the members of the FTC's House and Senate oversight committees and the location of the headquarters office of the various acquiring firms in the sample. A match was assumed for any Congressman or Senator representing the state in which the firm had its headquarters. Variables were calculated for both the subcommittee and full committee in both the House and Senate. In addition to reviewing the effects of each committee, one could add the representation at either the subcommittee or committee for both the House and the Senate to get an average measure of the "pork barrel" effect.[14] If the Commission responded to these "pork barrel" concerns a positive effect would be observed.

B. Summary of the Data

To set a background for the analysis, we present a brief overview of the data. Summary information on win rates organized by the merits variables is presented first, followed by an initial analysis of the relationships between case outcomes and the internal political factors. The section concludes with a look at the relationship between win rates and the external political considerations.

Table 1 presents the FTC win rate for the three types of cases (horizontal, vertical and potential competition) and three classifications of the competitive merits. Data are presented for both the pre-*General Dynamics* and the post-*General Dynamics* periods, with cells based on fewer than five cases marked with an asterisk. Win rates are lowest for potential competition cases and (surprisingly) highest

---

[13] On occasion, the transactions involved competitive concerns in more than one market (10 cases) or involved more than one challenged deal (12 cases). For those cases involving more than one market, the economic data were collected for the most serious overlap, while for cases involving more than one deal, the economic variables implicitly proxy a combined transaction. Likewise, the value of the deal represented the sum of all the transaction prices.

[14] Data at the committee chairman level was not used, because few firms would be represented by a chairman and data for the entire house or senate was not used, because almost all firms are represented by a congressman or senator (foreign firms would not represented by anyone.)

for vertical mergers. However, few vertical cases are included in the post-*General Dynamics* data, so no strong conclusions should be drawn. The link between merits and success is clear. In the three categories of cases, evidence on barriers to entry improves the likelihood of an injunction, and evidence of high concentration (greater than 2000) usually enhances the chance of success. Overall, the initial review of the data is compatible with our hypotheses that high barriers and Herfindahl findings are likely to lead to an injunction, and that potential competition cases are more likely to lead to dismissal, but casts a little doubt on the expectation for vertical cases.

It is possible to search for a relationship between either the number of "OLD" commissioners or the political affiliation of the Commissioners and the likelihood of a Commission merger order.[15] To start the analysis, cases are organized into five classifications, one for each of the last five Presidential eras. Given continuity of policy as Vice-Presidents replace Presidents, the length of the periods range from four years in the Carter administration to twelve years for the Reagan administration. These periods are defined by the time the President's party obtains control of the FTC, generally a year after the Presidential Inauguration, until the time the President's party loses control of the agency, again a year after the Inauguration.[16] Although the exact date associated with the switch in control is difficult to identify, very few cases are decided during a change in administrations.

Table 2 presents a summary of winning percentages classified by Presidential era and number of "OLD" commissioners. A number of observations can be made with the data. First, only one Reagan and no Carter era decisions involve three or more Commissioners that served when the case was initiated. This suggests either more Commission turnover or longer trial and appeal times. Second, the sample averages tend to suggest that the FTC was highly prone to find for itself until the Carter era.

---

[15] Information is also available for the relationship between the ALJ and final FTC decision. In general, the Commission upholds the ALJ decision (36 of 50 orders and 13 of 20 dismissals.) However, the Commission reversed the ALJ decision in thirty percent of the cases, with liability found in two-thirds of these decisions.

[16] The Clinton administration obtained effective control of the FTC in early 1995, two years into the Presidential term. However, this delay appears linked to an unusual pattern in the expiration of the Commissioners' terms and the lack of any Commission resignations.

Finally, the overall win rate appears to increase with the number of "OLD" commissioners. If one or two commissioners served on the prosecuting commission, the win rate averages around 60 percent. On the other hand, if three or more Commissioners served on the prosecuting commission, the win rate exceeds 90 percent.

A similar analysis can be undertaken for the political orientation of the Commission. Table 3 illustrates the winning percentage by Presidential era and percentage of Republicans on the deciding panel. While it is difficult to see any political effect in the Eisenhower, Kennedy, Nixon and Carter eras, the Reagan cases seem to show a decline in the likelihood of an order as the number of Republicans on the Commission increases. Moreover, the same general pattern appears to emerge in the overall data.

FTC winning percentages can also be organized by the political control of Congress. Table 4 is based on congressional data on various Senate and House oversight bodies organized into four categories. A congressional entity is considered conservative if the median ADA rating is less than 40, moderately conservative if the ADA rating is between 40 and 50, moderately liberal if the ADA rating is between 50 and 60 and liberal if the ADA rating is over 60. Senate and House ADA data for four classifications, the entire chamber, the committee, the subcommittee and the subcommittee chairman are used in the analysis. Average winning percentages for FTC cases are computed for each cell in the table, with percentages based on fewer than five observations marked with an asterisk. Abstracting from the small sample cases, the Senate data generally shows the expected rise in success rates with the ADA rating. This effect is more noticeable for the various committee and subcommittee levels, and significantly less obvious at the full senate level. The House results are much more confusing, with no clear pattern emerging. This may be caused by the fact that 89 percent of the cases were decided under oversight from liberal (as defined above) subcommittee chairmen. If these individuals had the relevant political power, then there may not be enough variance in the data to identify any effect. Overall, while it is likely any Senate effect can be identified, a House effect may not be observed in the data.

11

A final test would replicate the Faith, Leavens and Tollison test. The winning percentage of the firms with "representation" in Congressional committees was actually lower than the winning percentage of the control group (although the result was only significant for the Senate subcommittee). Thus, the initial review of the data does not support the pork barrel hypothesis.

In general, the initial analyses of the data are suggestive of a number of our hypothesized findings, but more detailed analyses is necessary before any strong conclusions are drawn. Thus, we turn to an econometric model of FTC decision making to investigate the various findings.

IV. ESTIMATION RESULTS

A statistical model will be presented here to attempt to explain the Commission's win rate as a function of the various independent variables. Since the FTC can either rule for or against itself on a particular case, the relevant dependent variable will be binomial, that is, either 0 or 1. Therefore, a limited dependent variable estimator such as the probit is an appropriate procedure for this econometric question. We analyze the data in two steps. First, we estimate probit coefficients for the merits and internal political variables and then we estimate a larger model that adds external political variables.

To set the background for the probit analyses, Table 5 calculates means for all the relevant variables for the period 1950-1974 (the pre-*General Dynamics* era), 1974-1992 (the post-*General Dynamics* era) and the entire sample. Although some differences were observed, a number of other variables were almost identical over the entire period.

The average Herfindahl was generally the same over the entire period, a result which was also observed when the sample is limited to horizontal mergers. Barriers to entry were found in roughly 70 percent of the cases in each subperiod. More recent cases appear to have shifted away from vertical mergers, with the percentage of vertical challenges significantly lower in the post-*General Dynamics* period.

The internal political variables show the same mixed results. Early cases were heard by an average of 2.19 "OLD" commissioners, while relatively recent cases had a significantly smaller average

12

of 1.56. On the other hand, the variable proxying the average political affiliation of the commissioners, Republican, remained largely the same over the two eras. The other political variable, defined by the party of the President that appointed the commissioners, identified a significant swing towards the Republican party which matches the change in White House control over the two eras.

Overall, the cases tend to involve both larger firms and transactions after 1974, with the difference significant for both sales of the acquiring firm and the value of the transaction. Also, the Congressional variables picked up the change in political control representative of the overall data. While the relevant Senate variables tended to become more conservative (lower ADA ranking), the House appeared more liberal, especially at the oversight committee. Finally, the pork variables identified the fact that acquiring firms tended to be more likely to have representation on oversight subcommittees before the General Dyanamics decision than after. This result did not occur for the overall committee and probably adds little to the analysis.

Three sets of probit coefficients are estimated in Table 6, the first of which considers the merits variables, the second which adds a number of internal political factors, and a third which uses a narrower set of internal political factors. The merits and internal factors are generally significant, regardless of the specification of the model.

The first column of results in Table 6 reports the relevant coefficients for a pure "merits" model. We find that the coefficients on the two merits variables, Herfindahl and Barriers, have the expected signs and the barrier variable is clearly significant. Other coefficients suggest that potential competition cases face higher standards than the horizontal cases, while the standards for vertical cases do not appear to be different from the horizontal cases. The results also indicate that the Commission standards were relaxed after the *General Dynamics* decision.[17]

---

[17] While the limited data preclude an exact test, the explanatory power of the time trend model exceeds that of a model incorporating only a dummy variable for the 1974 *General Dynamics* decision.

The second column highlights the results of a broad "merits and internal politics" model. Of perhaps greatest interest is the coefficient for the number of "OLD" Commissioners. The positive sign of this variable indicates that commissioners are more likely to vote for administrative complaints if they were members of the commission that chose to prosecute those cases. Thus, it appears to matter if Commissioners act as both prosecutors and judges.

The coefficient on the party affiliation variable, Republican, has the expected sign and is statistically significant, indicating that the political composition of the commission impacts on merger decisions.[18] In particular, as Republicans replace Democrats, the commission becomes relatively less likely to enjoin a transaction. The coefficient on the variable for the political party appointing the Commissioner, President, however, is insignificant (and takes on an opposite sign than what was expected.) Therefore, the party of the President making the appointment does not appear to be relevant.[19] Given the FTC Act prevents one party from obtaining more than three seats on the Commission, it is possible that the Senate's confirmation process precludes the President from appointing members from the opposition party that are too far out of step with the opposition party's mainstream viewpoint. Thus, for example, Democrats appointed by a Republican president would tend to vote like Democrats.[20]

We reestimated the model without the weak political variable (President) and the results are reported in the third column. While the explanatory power of the model falls slightly, the similarity of the coefficients suggests the basic results are robust to the exact specification of the model.

External political variables for firm size and congressional ideology are added to the final model of Column 3 (Table 6) to generate the results in Table 7. Four formulations of the case-specific

---

[18] The significance of both variables increases dramatically if date is deleted from the model.

[19] The President variable is not significant if the Republican variable is omitted from the model to minimize the potential for multicollinearity.

[20] An alternative explanation is that individuals appointed to the Commission vote to please their party to assure consideration for future jobs once their current term expires. In effect, the views of the appointee change once appointed to the Commission.

political variable are matched with four formulations of the Congressional variables to check for the robustness of the results. In particular, both the real value of the acquiring party's sales and the real value of the transaction (in either dollars or logarithmic form) are considered as measuring general political effects. Likewise, the Congressional control variables are measured at the entire house, the committee, the subcommittee and subcommittee chairman level as noted in the table. While this approach generates a total of 16 possibilities, a representative four are presented for analysis.

Overall, the merits variables (Herfindahl and Barriers) retain their explanatory power when the model is generalized to consider external political forces. Potential competition cases remain statistically less likely than horizontal cases to result in Commission orders and vertical cases appear less likely in one of the four models. Overall, the merits still matter in the presence of exogenous political variables.

The internal political variables also appear to retain significance, although the conclusion is not as strong. One formulation of the exogenous political variables eliminates the significance of the "OLD" commissioners and another the significance of politics. Moreover, the coefficient for OLD commissioners is only marginally significant in the other regressions.[21]

Interesting, few of the political variables show any statistical significance. The transaction-related variables (price and sales) tended to reduce the likelihood of a merger order, but were insignificant. Moreover, of all the formulations of the congressional variables, only the House subcommittee chairman has a clear effect on the decision process and the sign is negative, indicating a more liberal chairman reduces the likelihood of a Commission order. It is difficult to place much credence in this result.[22]

---

[21] The coefficient does reach a standard significance level in three of the 16 runs. Moreover, the significance of the coefficient improves for other specifications of the model.

[22] Significant results tend to be obtained for the Senate subcommittee and subcommittee chairman if the time shift parameter is removed from the model. This choice would appear inappropriate, because the shift is necessary to account for a change in legal standards. The significant Senate result may be caused by a contemporaneous conservative shift in the Senate oversight subcommittee in the mid 1970's.

This outline is slightly surprising given our tabulations and the previous research showing a relationship between Congressional control and FTC decisions. One possibility is the addition of the internal political variables to the model capture political effects linked to Congressional factors. Another possibility is the longer time period (1956-1992) obscures a Congressional power that ebbs and flows between the Senate and the House and among the various committee groups. While focusing on smaller periods of time could minimize this problem, it would create another problem associated with small samples.[23]

Table 8 reports our test of the pork barrel hypothesis. The first model of Table 8 uses the number of relevant congressmen and senators on the FTC's oversight subcommittee, while the second model uses the number on the oversight committee. The pork barrel coefficient is not significant in either of these specifications, nor in any of the several other specifications we attempted. This result suggests the earlier support for the pork barrel hypthesis cannot be replicated in a more general model over a broader time period. Again while smaller time periods could be studied, the lack of data makes this approach difficult.

The merits-internal political model in Column 3 of Table 6 appears to be the most appropriate equation for predicting Commission decisions. For a horizontal merger case, with the "OLD" commissioners and Republican variables at their means and the time index set to June 1995, we find the presence of barriers can raise the probability of an order from 5 percent to 87 percent for a Herfindahl of 3000. Changes in the Herfindahl have smaller effects, with a Herfindahl of 2000 associated with a 75 percent change of an order and a Herfindahl of 4000 linked to a 95 percent chance of an order.

Internal political variables also have an impact on the outcome of the case. For a horizontal decision in June 1995 that finds barriers to entry and a Herfindahl of 2000, the probability of an order can range from 24 percent for a Commission controlled by Republicans and no "OLD" commissioners

---

[23] If one introduces a shift variable to allow the coefficient on the Senate and House variables to change after the *General Dynamics* decision, one finds a significant positive effect on the Senate and subcommittee ADA rating and a significant negative effect on the House and subcommittee rating for the post 1974 period. These results cannot be replicated with the post-1974 sample.

to 96 percent for a Commission dominated by Democrats and three old Commissioners. However, these bounds are somewhat unrealistic, because a Commission in transition from one party to the other is unlikely to have many "OLD" commissioners. Given the remaining terms of actual Commissioners, it is likely to be dominated by Democrats, but with one or two "OLD" commissioners. This would suggest a probability of a Commission order against the merger under discussion of between 78 and 90 percent. Overall, the model suggests that both the merits and internal politics are extremely important in the outcome of merger cases.

V.   CONCLUSION

Our review of FTC administrative decision making generate a number of interesting initial conclusions. The mix of cases appears to have changed over time, with a movement away from vertical and potential competition mergers. Winning percentages were initially high, but fell in the 1970 Econometrics results indicate that both the economic merits and internal political factors affect Commission merger decisions. In particular, the ability of commissioners to act as both prosecutor and judge on a particular matter can significantly increase the likelihood of a merger order. Likewise, a Republican-dominated Commission appears less likely to oppose a transaction. Somewhat surprisingly, however, we were unable to find on impact of external political factors on the FTC's decisions.

While the statistical significance of the number of "OLD" Commissioners suggests an internal political problem with the administrative process, the political variables clearly suggest that the FTC Act has been successful in achieving some political balance at the Commission. Abstracting from personalities, Democratic (Republican) appointees of Republican (Democratic) Presidents tend to vote similar to Democratic (Republican) appointees of Democratic (Republican) Presidents. In contrast to previous studies, however, external political orientations or pork barrel considerations do not appear to significantly influence judicial decisions of the FTC.

Table 1

FTC Win Rates by Type of Case and Merits
(before and after General Dynamics' Decision)

	1950 - 74	1974 - 92	Total	Cases
Horizontal				44
0	75	29	53	15
1 - 2000	100	64	75	16
2000+	100	83	92	13
Average	90	58	73	
Vertical				12
0	0*	-	0*	2
1 - 2000	100*	100*	100	5
2000+	100*	100*	100	5
Average	80	100*	83	
Potential				14
0	0*	0*	0*	4
1 - 2000	100*	50*	67*	3
2000+	100*	67*	86	7
Average	83	38	57	

*Less than 5 cases in a cell

Table 2

Winning Percentages by Number of "Old" Commissioners

Number of "Old" Commissioners

FTC Era	0	1	2	3	4	5	Mean
Ike	100	100	100	100	100	-	100
Kennedy	100	57	-	100	100	100	84
Nixon	-	67	80	86	100	-	80
Carter	-	75	50	-	-	-	63
Reagan	0	50	37.5	0	-	-	38
Overall	83	63	58	87	100	100	71
Cases	6	24	19	15	5	1	

FTC Eras

Ike   1954 - 1961
Kennedy   1962 - 1969
Nixon   1970 - 1977
Carter   1978 - 1981
Reagan   1982 - 1992

Table 3

Winning Percentage by Average Political Affiliation of Commission

Percentage of Republicans

FTC Era	.25	.33	.40	.50	.60	.67	.75	Mean
Ike	-	-	100	100	100	-	100	100
Kennedy	-	100	67	100	-	100	-	84
Nixon	-	100	100	80	75	100	-	80
Carter	67	-	33	100	-	-	-	63
Reagan	-	-	-	50	29	50	33	38
Overall	67	100	64	88	64	67	50	71
Cases	3	4	14	17	22	6	4	

Table 4

Winning Percentages by Type of Political Control

	Senate	Committee	Subcommittee	Chairman
Conservative	64	59	45	41
Moderate - C	73	70	73	100*
Moderate - L	75	75	58	88
Liberal	50*	100	92	79

	House	Committee	Subcommittee	Chairman
Conservative	75	78	77	100*
Moderate - C	85	71	83	100*
Moderate - L	55	71	58	100*
Liberal	-	33	65	68

* Less than 5 cases in class

Conservative	ADA < 40
Moderate - C	$40 \leq ADA < 50$
Moderate - L	$50 \leq ADA < 60$
Liberal	$60 \leq ADA$

ADA - Americans for Democratic Action Congressional Vote Rating

Table 5

Means of the Variables

	1950 - 1974	1974 - 1992	Total
Merit Variables			
Herfindahl	2622	2216	2425
Barriers	.69	.71	.70
Vertical	.28	.06*	.17
Pot. Comp.	.17	.24	.20
Internal Politics			
Old Comm.	2.19	1.56*	1.89
Republican	.51	.53	.52
President	.33	.63*	.48
External Politics			
Sales	1.83	2.98*	2.39
Price	3.41	4.46*	3.92
Senate (ADA)	49.2	46.6	48.0
Committee	52.0	40.9*	46.6
Subcommittee	60.3	43.0*	51.9
Chairman	77.4	41.0*	59.7
House (ADA)	40.3	44.3*	42.2
Committee	29.6	51.9*	40.5
Subcommittee	47.6	47.8	47.7
Chairman	85.5	70.3*	78.1
Subcommittee Pork	.78	.44*	.61
Committee Pork	2.30	2.24	2.27

* The difference between the two periods is significant.

Table 6

Regression Results - Merits and Internal Politics Models
(t-statistics in parentheses)

Variable	Merits Model	Merits & Internal Model (I)	Merits & Internal Model (II)
Constant	0.771 (0.14)	1.02 (0.85)	0.944 (.80)
Herfindahl	0.000285 (1.51)	.000499 (1.88)	.000479 (1.83)
Barriers	2.20 (3.82)	2.78 (3.66)	2.81 (3.74)
Vertical	-.815 (-1.17)	-0.841 (-1.10)	-0.884 (-1.17)
Pot. Comp.	-1.13 (-1.85)	-1.44 (-1.80)	-1.47 (-1.82)
Time Shift	-0.00610 (-3.30)	-0.00587 (-2.58)	-0.00542 (-2.67)
Old Comm.	-	0.541 (1.71)	0.525 (1.66)
Republican	-	-5.41 (-2.00)	-4.76 (-2.05)
President	-	.564 (.48)	-
Adj R-Square	.478	.572	.565
Success Rate	84.2%	91.4%	90.0%
Log Likelihood	-22.53	-19.01	-19.13

Table 7

Regression Results - External Political Models
(t-statistics in parentheses)

Variable	Sales,Full House Model	Log Sales, Committee Model	Price, Sub-committee Model	Log Price, Subcommittee Chair Model
Constant	0.958 (.46)	1.12 (0.60)	1.85 (.93)	4.72 (1.84)
Herfindahl	.000566 (1.78)	.000477 (1.77)	.000610 (1.98)	.000597 (1.81)
Barrier	2.91 (3.75)	2.94 (3.81)	3.48 (3.33)	3.91 (3.25)
Vertical	-0.944 (-1.16)	-0.847 (-1.07)	-1.16 (-1.25)	-1.784 (-1.73)
Pot. Comp.	-1.49 (-1.74)	-1.26 (-1.53)	-1.96 (-2.17)	-1.78 (-1.91)
Time Shift	-0.00478 (-2.25)	-0.00503 (-1.64)	-0.00476 (-1.94)	-0.00765 (-2.27)
Old Comm.	0.510 (1.45)	0.564 (1.65)	0.260 (0.65)	0.584 (1.58)
Republican	-4.26 (-1.77)	-5.00 (-2.06)	-5.93 (-2.20)	-2.80 (-1.04)
Sales or Price	-.00482 (-.70)	-0.198 (-.88)	-.000994 (-1.21)	-0.276 (-1.28)
Senate Index	0.0157 (.48)	-0.00165 (-0.064)	0.0285 (1.20)	0.0111 (0.86)
House Index	-0.0266 (-0.79)	0.00705 (0.29)	-0.0325 (-1.63)	-0.0582 (-2.36)
Adj. R-Square	.577	.592	.630	.697
Success Rate	88.6%	91.4%	90.0%	91.4%
Log Likelihood	-18.43	-18.62	-16.36	-14.19

Table 8
Regression Results - Pork Barrel Model

Variable	Subcommittee Number	Committee Number
Constant	0.735 (0.587)	0.649 (0.486)
Herfindahl	.00495 (1.88)	.00485 (1.84)
Barrier	2.805 (3.73)	2.730 (3.59)
Vertical	-0.762 (-0.953)	-0.807 (-1.05)
Pot. Corp.	-1.402 (-1.73)	-1.340 (-1.61)
Time Shift	-.0504 (-2.36)	-.0515 (-2.49)
Old Comm.	0.553 (1.72)	0.510 (1.64)
Republican	-4.87 (-2.06)	-4.653 (-1.96)
Pork Barrel Index	0.156 (0.48)	.0941 (0.48)
Adj. R-Square	0.576	0.571
Success Rate	92.8%	90.0%
Log Likelihood	-19.02	-19.02

REFERENCES

Coate, Malcolm B., Richard S. Higgins and Fred S. McChesney, "Bureaucracy and Politics in FTC Merger Challenges," Journal of Law and Economics 33(2) (October 1990) 463-482.

Coate, Malcolm B., Andrew N. Kleit and Rene Bustamante, "Fight, Fold or Settle?: Modelling the Reaction to FTC Merger Challenges," Economic Inquiry 33:4 (forthcoming, October 1995).

Cohen, Mark A., "Explaining Judicial Behavior or What's "Unconstitutional" About the Sentencing Commission," Journal of Law, Economics, and Organization 7:1 (1991) 183-199.

Faith, Roger L., Donald R. Leavens, and Robert D. Tollison, "Antitrust Pork Barrel," Journal of Law and Economics 15:2 (October 1982) 329-42.

McChesney, Fred S., "Rent Extraction and Rent Creation in the Economic Theory of Regulation," Journal of Legal Studies 20(1) (1991) 73-93.

Posner, Richard A., "The Federal Trade Commission," University of Chicago Law Review 37(1) (1969) 47-89.

Posner, Richard A., "The Federal Trade Commission," University of Chicago Law Review 47(1) (1967) 47-97.

"Report of the American Bar Association Section on Antitrust Law," Antitrust Trade and Regulation Report, No. 1410, (April 6, 1989).

Spiller, Pablo T., and Rafael Gely, "Congressional Control or Judicial Independence? The Determinants of U.S. Supreme Court Labor-Relations Decisions, 1949-1988," Rand Journal of Economics 23(4) (Winter 1992) 463-492.

Weingast, Barry J., and Mark J. Moran, "Bureaucratic Discretion or Congressional Control? Regulatory Policymaking at the Federal Trade Commission," Journal of Political Economy 91 (1983) 765-800.

U.S. Department of Justice, "Department of Justice and Federal Trade Commission Horizontal Merger Guidelines," Antitrust Trade and Regulation Report, No. 1559, (April 2, 1992).

www.ingramcontent.com/pod-product-compliance
Lightning Source LLC
Chambersburg PA
CBHW081249170526
45165CB00009B/3261